Girl after Girl after Girl

BARATARIA POETRY SERIES

Ava Leavell Haymon, *Series Editor*

Girl after Girl after Girl

Poems

Nicole Cooley

Louisiana State University Press
Baton Rouge

Published by Louisiana State University Press

Manufactured in the United States of America
First printing

DESIGNER: *Mandy McDonald Scallan*
TYPEFACE: *Whitman, text; Charcuterie Contrast, display*
PRINTER AND BINDER: *McNaughton & Gunn, Inc*

Library of Congress Cataloging-in-Publication Data
Names: Cooley, Nicole, author.
Title: Girl after girl after girl : poems / Nicole Cooley.
Description: Baton Rouge : Louisiana State University Press, 2017. | Series: Barataria poetry series
Identifiers: LCCN 2017005130| ISBN 978-0-8071-6683-3 (pbk. : alk. paper) | ISBN 978-0-8071-6684-0 (pdf) | ISBN 978-0-8071-6685-7 (epub)
Classification: LCC PS3553.O5647 A6 2017 | DDC 811/.5—dc23
LC record available at https://lccn.loc.gov/2017005130

The paper in this book meets the guidelines for permanence and durability of the Committee on Production Guidelines for Book Longevity of the Council on Library Resources. ♾

For Meridian

Iris   my first girl   of fairy tales and
orange clouds   baby quilt pulled tight
to cover us   girl who made me a mother

For Arcadia

Rose   my dandelion   my field of wild
violets   my little flip book baby
girl who made one into two   now sisters

A light white, a disgrace, an ink spot, a rosy charm.

—GERTRUDE STEIN, *Tender Buttons: Objects, Food, Rooms*

Here, indeed, lies the whole miracle of collecting. For it is invariably oneself that one collects.

—JEAN BAUDRILLARD, "The System of Collecting"

Contents

I.
Of Collection

a gathering of objects or of persons, as works of art; a quantity of anything collected together into a mass; an assemblage

see also, 1460; of floating vapors, 1747; of waters

stamp collection; coin collection; collection of rainwater

aggregation   assemblage   pharmacopoeia

I want to float in vapors—in a slow, dark rain

No—I want to climb inside this album of coins

to turn myself into the tiniest, the most worthless,
to slip inside the silver skin of a dime

stockpile   hoard   archive

heap of girls laughing on a bed

request for a sum of money

a mass in a body

in the herbarium: a veined plant is a daughter's ribcage

Mad Money

When I find my mother's jewelry box—blonde leather, impossibly
fifties teenage—desire fills my chest like dirty

shredded Kleenex—desire for my mother's sixteen-year-old self.

Beside the place for pearls: a drawer labeled *Mad Money.*
Inside the drawer, a blue soap crumbled to dust

and three nickels I set in my mouth, wanting silver bitterness.

Money she saved so she could run away?
From my father?—

The first *nostalgics* were men at war: mercenaries
in the French army longing for their villages.

Originally a medical condition—
In the eighteenth century: *severe homesickness,* a disease.

Nostalgia, from German *heimweh,* Greek *nostos* "homecoming"
+ *algos* "pain, grief."

My nostalgia is never a lovely wishing but instead
soldiers marching through yellow fields, dizzy with nausea.

When I open her jewelry box, I want to lie
in my mother's twin bed, on clean white sheets, to let go

of my body, to become the girl she was, mother-not-mother—

Under my tongue, her coins are cool and slick,
and I'm sick for a home I never lived in.

I slip on my mother's pink coat from high school,
color of a Dairy-Queen dipped cone,

color of a flushed cheek after a slap—

The S&H Green Stamp Book

1.

My mother believes in saving, in pasting
pinky-sheared edges of the stamps into the books.

On the fabric cutting board, in bed at night, she teaches
us how to rip the stamps into strips, lick and stick them

in the Gift Saver book. My father gone. My father at the bar,
my father breaking down the door to our bedroom.

The three of us inside.

2.

Each night I tell my daughters,
Do you understand I'll never leave you?
Stop asking that, my older daughter shudders, turns away.

3.

Once upon a time,
the wolf skittered down a chimney,
into a boiling pot.

Once upon a time,
girls hid from him,
his low persistent growl
in the kitchen.

4.

The stamps make me want to swallow and swallow.
The stamps are a puzzle of non-language my sister and I arrange
on our bed. The stamps are pleasure in counting.

5.

Have a second child, the poet told me. She herself a mother of one.
Without a second you are locked in a triangle.

6.

We're locked in: deadbolt shoved shut. Door won't splinter.

7.

I've always loved the math of it: one girl for each parent.
Two girls, heads bowed over the books of stamps,
pretending not to hear glass breaking.
Two daughters, so one could save the other.

8.

Now I'm the Mother. The one in the bedroom
with her daughters watching them sleep.
They wake up and tell me to go.
The one in the kitchen watching herself
knife through the breakfast toast.

9.

My mother must have believed she was saving us each time she left us at the airport all night to sit in slick black chairs, when she brought us to motels on Airline Highway and locked us in and drove back to our father.

We believed she would never come back.

10.

In the pot, the wolf churns, all body. But the wolf can climb out of the pot,
lift himself on his dirty grey paws, eyes glittering.

11.

Collecting: how many sheets of stamps, how many slick black chairs,
how many missing mothers—

Counting: the math of it: leave, don't leave.

[Baby's Cradle, Europe c. 1810]

A separate bed prevented babies being accidentally smothered by a parent—

The wicker cradle can't hold the baby, but it is just the right weight
for torn bits of lace,
a handful of sequins, a single loop of thread.

The baby can sleep in the icebox, the wooden chest down in the kitchen.
Its top flips open to silver like a grinning mouth.

The baby will be cold and quiet.

—with no secure mechanism to prevent over-rocking, babies often fell out
on to the floor or worse still into a nearby fireplace—

The Cocktail, A History

GIN PALACE

The olive floats in the glass like a moon.
Dark-red center I thought was rot
or an eye, watching my father.

Glass pearled with cold in his hand,
Martini's Holy Trinity in a triangular glass,
gin, vermouth, the twist, recipe

he taught us in childhood. Now
he has already left me to find the drink's pure
dry taste like the shoulder of a woman

who feels nothing when you touch her,
a woman in a white dress, choker of ice
circling her neck, the real happiness.

On the other side of the room, alone,
I build a castle of glasses, crystal
skyline. The tower a silver canister, the children's

rooms a shot glass. Inside, the family is all
reflections. Multiplied a thousand times
they can't recognize each other.

Older than the photograph,
the cocktail is a drink with a history.
A father named it.
Conjure up a story:
The princess Coctel is twelve, mixing drinks
for her father's guests, a feather
stuck in every glass.
Tray in her hand, she curtsies
spreading the skirt of her white dress.

Conjure up a story:
The King's voice is slurred.
His daughter is terrified.

In the twentieth century, other fathers invent drink names:
American Beauty. Maiden's Prayer.
Fallen Angel. Philomela. Mary Pickford.
White Witch.

YOUR BRIDE

When she opens her dress, inside she is all glass,
bottle after bottle hung from her neck,
her breasts, shimmering.
In the half-dark of your room, she is your angel,
her body a hall of mirrors.
Where is her sadness?
She'll pour you anything you want.
She'll lead you outside to a garden,
row of toothpicks flaring into flame.

SHIRLEY TEMPLE

At twelve, my sister pours witch hazel on ice.
I fill a shot glass to the top with turpentine.

Years ago we refused the cup of grape juice,
Christ's blood, sweet and thick, swallowed at the altar,

to drink the way soldiers drank during the war:
blood-red Mercurochrome, Aqua Velva, Mr. Clean.

Anything stinging the tongue, anything dangerous.

Years ago we named the family of dolls after
cocktails—Fallen Angel, White Witch—and gave up

the parasol stuck in the glass, the children's drink
with its bells of ice, pink and filtered with sugar.

Give American Beauty a medicine dropper of vermouth.
Her glass eyes roll closed as we hold her head still.

RECIPE: RAMOS GIN FIZZ

The drink named for the man whose house we rented
in New Orleans,
named for the house
where my father stepped through
the glass door, shattering the panes.

1½ ounces gin
1 tablespoon powdered sugar
3–4 drops orange flower water
juice of ½ lime
juice of ½ lemon
1 egg white
1 ½ ounces cream
1 squirt seltzer

The house where cream pooled on the table,
the orange flower water
too sweet to drink,

the house where a key cranked the ice machine
to foam the silver pitcher
with a magic potion I believed in.
I was not allowed to taste it.

Burn the twist of lemon over the drink's surface
till you're left with an oily slick.

where I sit now, on a block of crystal,

dull-white mirror. I take up a pick,
a mallet, to crack the past,

crush the family to pieces,
break all the father's bottles.

When I go back to childhood,
my hands shake with cold

and American Beauty is forever
a young girl, who lies on an ice bed,

already numb and anesthetized and blank.

[Breast Pump, c. 1905]

My nipples sting in memory.

I want to put the globe of blown glass
in my mouth.

—allowing a baby to be fed by carers other than the mother
or letting an afflicted mother rest—

as I remember leaning over my writing desk, becoming both
body and machine, both skin and suction funnel,

while the baby cries downstairs.

Now I feel it again: black tube snaking into the pump's sucking,
that blind grasp.

From My Mother's Copy of Peg Bracken's *I Hate To Cook Book* (1960)

SWOOP STEAK

I set *the round steak in a Dutch oven or a similar heavy iron skillet with a lid.* I slam the lid down. I lock it tight in place. Dutch oven the perfect size for a casket for my daughter's Little Mommy Dream Doll.

Now we'd better let that recipe rest.

What if I don't want to rest? What if I'm forever restless?

⁂

HORSERADISH BRISKET

I want to choke on stringy meat.
I want to grind coarse pepper
between my back teeth.

Immolate: Latin immolates, to sprinkle with meal before sacrificing, sacrifice, sacrificial barley cake, literally, millstone first use 15th century.

I want to burn my house down.

⁂

POT-ROAST BUNS

Which are good and not much trouble. Start with *two cups of beef bits.* Don't tell me you have no idea what that is. Don't tell me you don't know that vinegar is required. Don't forget a thin lemon slice to stick between your teeth. Don't tell me you don't love lemon's sour kiss.

⁂

ROSY MEATBALLS

I want a stain of red, my fingers lipsticked with beef and raw cold.

I am a bad example.

An 8-ounce can of tomato sauce and a 1-pound can
of whole cranberry sauce to pour over.

My dinner, flush as sex, flush as anger.

❧

SHOULDER BAGS

The recipe tells me I will *want to start with pieces.*
I tighten the foil around each fat pouch
like my babies I was taught to swaddle in pink blankets.

Salted and peppered lamb
A shoulder chop
A slice of onion
Pour a tablespoon of sherry on top   wrap up swiftly
so the sherry doesn't run out.

No, let the sherry run through my fingers.
I want to wash my hands in it,
to pour it over my wrists, my arms,
to lick it off my skin.

❧

CHIPPED BEEF ON TOAST

It's like money in the bank, that ever-ready jar of chipped beef,
waiting on the shelf

Is it money   is it fury   is it secret, hidden, in the oven?

Add a shot of cognac.

The Pregnant Doll

Ultrasound's shadowed green, slush and slur of a heartbeat—

but this doll's body is all plastic, the baby only visible if you remove
the doll's stomach, the size and color of a vanilla wafer.

Her stomach slides off neatly, the baby extracted
like a battery in the back of a clock.

It's not much like real life, the museum caption warns.
The baby never cries. The doll wears high heels and a nightgown

over her emptiness. She's thin in an instant. Never
an IV's bite and scrawl, never a monitor black-strapped on her skin,

never an injection into the cervix that doesn't work. She opens
easily, with a finger flick, then closes.

She's never a cut steak leaking blood onto a plate.
She's never birthsick or tired of being a household for another body.

Self-Portrait With Miniatures at the Victoria and Albert Museum

Animal bodies: vellum pasted to a playing card,

    smoothed with a burnisher built of a dog's tooth.

        Painted with a brush of squirrel hair.

The Elizabethan miniaturist Nicholas Hilliard recommended the skin
of an aborted calf, which was hairless and very smooth.

The room is cool and dark. Here is the squirrel. Here is the dog. The calf.

They moan and cry and nudge against my leg, they are babies
who want to be held, want to lay their heads against my shoulder,
want my lap, my arms, my mouth.

They cry and cry.

    I hold the magnifying glass up to the exhibit.

I want to be another girl's painted face

        shut tight in a locket.

Object Elegies

MY MOTHER'S BRIGHT-GREEN NYLON PANTIES

In New Orleans, fifth grade, Karen Beckman yanked up my skirt, told everyone, "Nicole's wearing go-go panties!" Made the boys all look. My mother had again not done the laundry, had given me hers. Three years later, Karen's father shot and killed the family while they slept then set the gun's body into his own mouth.

WATER LINE

When the older daughter cries, it starts as a wild quiet, then a slow leaking of her sadness into me, as we lie together on the wide bed, a spreading river, overtaking, soaking, until I am filled up. Like the black line at the roof of a ruined house after a hurricane—I wouldn't know the interior was lost unless my mother, who was driving me around New Orleans without my children, after the storm, pointed it out to me.

BETA FISH

We bury the younger daughter's fish in the backyard grass, under the trampoline, in a paper lunch bag. Fish killed by its sister. Fish the size of a rind of lime stuck on the edge of a glass. When I was first pregnant, the doctor said, *The baby is the size of a California strawberry!* She meant to comfort. I could not stop picturing it—a sweet red clot—in my unreliable body.

HOSPITAL PAIN SCALE

The strip of paper in my hands had no words only faces, round circles, hairless and grim-lipped. When I tried to answer, the nurse told me quickly, *That's for children.* When I tried to measure.

THE QUEEN OF HEARTS AS SEEN BY ALICE IN THE BOOK I READ TO MY DAUGHTER

Said to have *a crimson fury*, she cannot be mother or wife. The Queen with her scab-colored cheeks, her playing card sandwich-boarded over her breasts. The baby screams in her arms. The baby always screams. The Queen holds the mallet. Croquet, she knows, is all about *dead balls.*

ROCKING CHAIR

I'm not talking about where I sat and nursed the babies where they latched and unlatched but about the chair at the library children's section that tipped and hit the daughter's head, broke open her scalp, sliced through her dark hair. I'm talking about the thin silver staples the nurse unlinked from her body weeks later, dropped into my hand like treasure.

SIPPY CUP

Two-handled, he's a small fat man, the baby grabs him by his hips and bangs his body against her teeth, crushes him to her chest. Bangs him harder. She cries and cries in her blue stroller till I throw him to the sidewalk and he spins away, far from her, he's already gone, under a bus, under a bridge, smashed by traffic on Queens Boulevard.

EASTER EGG

Someone blew out the fragile shell of your daughter's egg and stuffed it with cigarette ashes. Dip it in vinegar flavored with the pink and yellow tablets, bad aspirin that could kill a child. Or make it sexy: fill the shell with dusting powder, puff shaped like a breast.

II.
Of Saving

of preservation from danger or destruction

—a cold glass doorknob like a fist—

of economizing

of being a good housekeeper!

once upon a time, a husband forced a wife's jaws apart
and poured in cool thin dimes
until she suffocated on her own money

of redeeming

of a lie like a hand covering a mouth

Resurrection Cake

Stir Jack Daniels, a pinch of salt, two sticks of butter, boxed cake mix
and canned fruit cocktail—

Pour more whiskey over the surface of the cake.

⁂

My grandmother crossing Western Avenue in Chicago on her way out of a bakery.
An accident: from *accidere,* to befall.

⁂

A leopard-print scarf to loop over her shoulders.

⁂

Bake in a Bundt cake pan, arrange
an empty grave, hill
for toothpick crosses, parsley trees.
With your best fondant, make Jesus' robe discarded.
Drop it near the empty place.

⁂

A no-bake version can be made with cereal and melted marshmallows.

⁂

My grandmother holding a white box full of what?—it is invisible—crullers,
cookies, sweet rolls.

My grandmother dead in an instant. Later at the bakery, the baker tells me,
I want you to know I stayed with her and whispered to her till the ambulance came.

❧

Box. Purse. She called it her *pocketbook.*

❧

Also called *The Empty Tomb Cake.*

❧

Inside her purse found later: leather low-heeled pumps kept never worn.
Inside: photo of her husband who died in 1955.

❧

Also called—*She is not here.*

I slide the cake in the oven. I stand beside her.

I'm holding a white box twined shut and stinking of sugar.

Floating Island

Whisking egg whites with two cold spoons with my daughter, in the kitchen,
the whites, most grotesque, most drawn-from-a-body, much worse

than yolks. The recipe requires meringue stiffened
into peaks that startle, that most resemble breasts.

My girl's bare feet beside mine on the black and white floor
while she scalds milk to thicken, slowly.

Do not let it form a skin, the recipe warns. What could live
inside milk skin? A scab, a patch of hair.

Also called *Eggs in Snow*. Also called *Birds Milk*.

I want *to layer alcohol-soaked dessert biscuits secretly inside*
but we are making a dessert to serve to daughters.

In the cookbook's photo, the Floating Island is a place
where I could rest, undisturbed, on a bed of egg whites, cool and dreamy,

like a pool of thin stretchy cervical mucus, to test ovulation,
—*I can't have another baby,* I explain—and then all the women I'll never be

line up beside me, aproned, wedding-dressed, tattooed.
With immersion blenders, apple corers, electric frying pans.

Also called *Ile Flottante*. In Serbia: *En Senockle*.

And under the milk skin is a baby, a baby I could pick up, hold,
swallow, my Thumbelina, my sweet homunculus,

who floats inside me like a piece of half-chewed gum.
The recipe warns, *Place the result in a very hot oven and don't take*

your eyes off it. Never, ever, take your eyes off any of it.

At the Corning Museum of Glass

First cake baked in glass

In the photograph, the other mother slits it
open proudly: her cake baked in a sawed-off

battery jar. At the table, her daughters
smile, toast the invention of the temperature tolerant.
A triangle slice for each: make your wartime meals
the best you've ever tasted!

I study the other mother's children while my daughter
jerks herself out of my arms, runs past me down the hall.

❧

end of the first year
end of layette now kept in a box in a basement
end of tiny hospital t-shirts
end of the socks that could fit on my finger
end of milk needling through my skin

❧

"Go away!" my daughter screams when I catch her as she buries
her head in my lap.

❧

In the photograph of the test kitchen I learn

that a cookbook holds more than a million recipes for glass,

written by good wife after good wife.

Pyrex is best:
add a frit of silicate, sand, soda
and ground lime.

Downstairs I follow my daughter—
a wake of cries and tantrumming and
an assembly line of baby bottles
winds before me like

a long sentence.

❧

A glass dress from the 1893 Chicago Columbian Exposition

Glass fibers break when touched, when a mother
angles the dress over a daughter's shoulders.

Dress of pain the mother put on the daughter.
Dress prickling, needling.

❧

all the daughter's first year:
cold spoon I held against her gums for teething
on her milk-blistered lips

❧

At the glass-blowing show, beside me, on the bench,
her shoes knock my legs, over and over
as we watch a glass river run through with light.

I watched her, newborn, to keep her breathing,
in a room lit pink like the bubble of glass
spinning before us now, iridescent,

pale and shimmering as the inside of a mouth, and how I wish
I could swallow her back down—this baby who is not a baby walking,
bring her back into my body, into that bubble of glass where she lived,

too hot, too still, too safe.

[Coral Rattle, 1650]

I picture the rattle on a silver-pink beach.

Lozenges of yellow light on the sea.

Sand sagging the toddler's pull-up.

Hurt me, my daughter says knowing nothing

about hurt while the sea hisses and spits at the shoreline.

Coral will stop gums bleeding. Coral will quit the crying.

Booklet, Hand-Pressed Paper, Containing Locks of Schoolchildren's Hair

Girls' hair wound on a bobbin like thread. Woven into a wreath

and cross-stitched with a sampler's background,
tiny heart-shaped flowers. All the hair collected

from the daughters who died of yellow fever, influenza.

I walk through the museum's hot dark,

past The Maori Warrior: an Ethnological Attraction.

Past the London Fat Man.
        The Dental Practice Head.

Where is the long table spread with loose strands
the mothers' hands straightening,
        unfurling curls to lay each flat?

In another century, a silver pitcher collects

water from the faucet with its sharp spout.

I stand at the sink and pour and pour, water running
through my daughter's long hair and down

her back, water that is all pleasure,

silver fistfuls over her skin.

❧

The daughters at their school desks,
penmanship booklets open to copy.

The daughters taken from their mothers.

The daughters in their beds, row upon row of white,
like a book's blank pages.

The daughters quarantined.

❧

I pour and pour as if water could make grief

small. As if I could wind it in a bobbin, hide it in a sewing box.

Hair wound. Unwound.

As if a silver mourning pin could ever close a mother's blouse

while her milk dries up, her breasts pinch shut.

Bye-Lo Baby, Patent Applied For

Baby in blue velvet, baby in fake lace.

Baby with lips set in a grim thin line.

Baby all celluloid, baby glass eyes stuck in her sockets.

Baby forever half-sleeping.

In the NICU, in an incubator, in the museum behind glass.

Bye-Lo Baby when invented first needed a model.

My baby,

not my baby,

baby I don't want,

baby I love best.

My daughters say: why can't you have another baby?

The inventor searched and searched. Hospital to hospital.

Baby, one eye open, baby watching from the corner, from the edge
of the bed.

Model baby! Baby three days old, baby copied.

Baby drawn—baby drawn and quartered?—Baby photographed.
Baby whose mother is where—

Baby patented. Baby made and made and made in a factory in Germany.

My daughters say, I want that baby! Make a baby for me!

All dressed-up baby, baby in her velvet, boxed up baby,

baby back-storied,

baby inventoried.

Another baby?

Lo Baby, Bye Baby, Baby Bye Bye at the bed side, museum baby, baby taken
from your mother's arms.

Vintage 1969 Mattel Baby Tender Love Doll, Talks, Drinks and Wets

Baby like a Magic 8-Ball. Baby like a boiled egg—

My real baby's cries fill the room. She could swallow the whole house
into her pink rosebud mouth. I've been told crying is her language.

I've been told to lock her alone in a room then bite down
on a towel to keep from screaming as she cries. Instead I remember

Baby Tender Love, doll baby who only speaks if you yank her string.
Obedient toddler: if you tip a bottle of fake milk to her mouth

she will neatly soak her diaper. I loved her and I want to buy this baby
now sold on eBay, I remember her mechanical voice,

I love you I love you I love you while I sit all night nursing
my real baby in my green rocking chair. Baby Chew My Finger.

Baby Tatter My Skin. *Sweet facial complexion with painted dark eyes.*
Short rooted hair ~ wearing this lovely knitted pink top, skirt and panties

First week of her life, I left my daughter only once, for infant CPR Class.
Bent over the rubber baby model, I bit the lip of the false baby hard as I could.

Baby Who Won't Sleep. Baby I Can't Put Down Because She'll Scream.
Crying is the way a baby roots herself to earth. Crying is her protest

at being born from me, her fury at being given me as her mother.
Baby Fingers Twined in My Hair. Baby Head Slick with Gel

for an Ultrasound on Her Brain. Baby Waiting With Me in Radiology in the Dark
Baby Sweet Yeast Smell Behind Her Knees.

In the middle of the night, in the green chair—Refuse Baby, Tattered Baby—
Baby Tender Love cries only once to tell me she is sick, to alert me

that the river of milk running fast through her bloodstream
is poison, that she wants me to twist the string tight

around her neck, thread an NG tube up her nose,
slip a bolus of morphine into her hand like an empty balloon,

glue a fentanyl patch to her thigh. Baby Be an Egg That Opens.
Dear Baby on My Lap. Dear toddler body I once loved.

Can you burn a plastic body down to ash?

[Swaddling Band, France, 18th Century]

After her birth, before they set her in my arms,

the nurses show me how to wrap the baby in her flannel,

how to swaddle,

how to bind her tightly, arms at her sides, legs pressed together,

how to turn her back into an object I can keep.

The Mannequin in the Mourning Dress at the Exhibition

is a new widow, in a black crepe dress and a spoon bonnet,

her gold jet memorial ring hidden on the wrong

finger, her locket twined with her husband's hair.

When I walk in the museum, all I can think

is that I love her dress: its fat pagoda sleeves, its trimmed velvet.

She is *a woman of sexual experience without marital constraints.*

In my slow circle alone
past all the mannequins, I learn

that the widow's baby is allowed to wear a white dress after a death,
small black bows

knotted at her shoulders, *as children of a certain age wear mourning white.*

Finally, I understand that a museum is like a hospital, a place of no

weather, place of no windows, except in a hospital no one

wants to look so my gazing would be forbidden—

In her mourning this new widow is not allowed to be lavish with grief—

Her dress: what dulled finish, faded mousseline and taffeta—

In a hospital now, all is lusterless,

and I lower my eyes, pretend to be invisible,

while *to be a Widow is to be fascinating and dangerous,* but to hide
that danger,

to shop in the Mourning Goods Store in search

   of a dress the color of eggplant, to request a single pleated skirt.

Not to remove your clothes, to unspool the hair in your necklace, to insist
on vivid

purple, on only true black, between your legs—

Object Elegies

ENGLISH IRONSTONE ADAMS CHINA SERVICE FOR EIGHT

I watch from the kitchen window as each girl swings, arm to arm, white tights flocked with mud, on the monkey bars, above the iced grass.

Three years after her death, I unpack the box of my grandmother's dishes, box of too much, too many. Plates, pitchers, sugar bowls, gravy boats. I crowd the cupboard, slam it closed. Open, remove, restack.

I hate winter's sunlight that leaks in through the kitchen windows. Girls wait at the table with teacups of milk. My girls, who never knew her. I take the new potatoes from the roasting pan, spoon them out on her cold blue saucers.

SILVER PORRINGER WITH FILIGREE, 1942

In the attic where my mother refused to save anything, on the floor, brushed sawdust clean, here is what's not: my father's silver baby bowl, with its lacy sterling handle, my grandmother filled with rice cereal, her baby's first meal.

QUILT WITH TATTED BORDER

An avocado pit lists in a glass on the bedroom sill, shape of an ovary, shape of an eye. And still I try to explain what things will last, to smooth out this expanse of fabric, to press my girl's fingers to the handiwork, to make her imagine someone's mother stitching and stitching the cloth I spread over her body. In my bed before she sleeps, my daughter whispers, *Shut up,* then moves closer.

SALT AND PEPPER SHAKERS IN THE SHAPE OF DUTCH GIRLS

White china suffers in the box till I set it on the table
beside a ring of butter soft as loose skin.

PINK PLASTIC CAKE BOX

I set the box, round as a pillbox hat, empty on the counter. I'll never make any cake that it will hold. Stunned eager pink.

SOUVENIR SPOONS MY GRANDMOTHER COLLECTED

From Phoenix From Atlantic City From San Francisco From Montreal From Puerto Rico From Bermuda

Carefully, my daughter sets them one on top of the other, each half circle cupping another.

RUBY GLASSES SET OF FOUR

I set one on each placemat beside a napkin cinched tight with ribbon.
Watch the goblets pinking with milk.
Ribbon cinched tight, red string tied on a wrist—to force my remembering.

CRYSTAL CHOKER

Yard sale Saturday, without our daughters, my friend and I walked through her town, stopping at card tables, knocking crystal and jet bead necklaces against our teeth to test for real glass or not. Transparent bubbles linked on string, heavy and cold on my throat, were what I craved most.

BAG OF DIARY KEYS

Jumbled like baby teeth in a box, now they crack and scatter. The pages they could open are all gone. Our secrets—my daughters and mine—

Here is what's not.

A COCKTAIL SHAKER I PLAN TO FILL WITH CRAYONS

Because I could only find one. Because it is painted with fruit, apples and oranges shaped like cherubs winding a garland. Because women are not supposed to drink alone. Because my grandmother would fill it with cold vodka and ice, and shake it and pour it out and sit at the edge of the river.

Because the edges of the glass are painted with lemons heavy as breasts, each a small bag of flesh.

C.

III.
Of Escape

to get away, as if by flight, to issue from confinement

to run wild from cultivation

to avoid a threatening evil

in my dream I'm wearing a paper dress   I'm alone
I'm running in the street

from Vulgar Latin excappare, from Latin ex-
+ Late Latin cappa head covering, cloak

to be outside the memory of

in my dream my white gloves are filled with ice

to fail to be remembered

Reticule

Small mouth like a gasp, fish caught on a hook, body all string,
meshed fabric bag in a century when pockets temporarily disappeared,

the *Reticule* also known as *Ridicule,* kept close to the body,
like my own shame, strung too tight in my chest.

The crocheted miser—you must fill it with German coins—
is a ring or finger purse, named after *pinch the penny.*

My saffron-colored knee socks shadowed with chalk,
I stand up from hot summer gravel where I have tried

to flatten my body into the ground, where the boy flattened
his body over mine by the river by the road by the scrub grass of the levee.

And a mother says, *girls, take note: you will need a buttonhook match safe*
for your loose matches and a striker. You will need a knife

that folds into a pencil to protect yourself,
a bottle of smelling salts with an easy screw-off top.

What if you need to get away from him?
You will need mad money, coins sewn into the hem of your dress.

You will need a purse worn under your skirt.
Do you think I'm talking about a body?

I'm talking about a celluloid notebook, a girl's locked diary.
Do you have your voice pastilles? Your St. Joseph's aspirin?

On my imaginary date, I wear pink plastic cats eyes,
wrist-length white cotton gloves. My mother says,

you should be ashamed. I should let myself dissolve,
in Bakelite, in Lucite, hide myself, plan out my escape,

make myself small and locked inside, snapped shut.

[Posture Board, England, 1820]

Nothing drowns out my girl's crying,
nothing quits the pinch in my throat,
fist thudding in my chest at my child's grief.

—This board has been inscribed with the names of five children who have used it—
Sally, Gatie, Tiny, Ada and Maud—

My girl's sobbing settles white cotton
over every table and chair,
as we leave the house.

—The board, positioned behind the back of the girl and held in place
by her arms, pulled the shoulders back—

On the way to the car, she whispers,
Don't make me go—
her fingers twist my hair, her fingers itch my skin.

I force her into her car seat,
lock plastic straps across her chest, while
her arms wind tight around my neck.

Frozen Charlottes, A Sequence

A Young Woman was frozen to death while riding to a ball.
—*The New York Observer,* January 1, 1840

Naked, arms molded to her sides, the doll can't move.
Drop her, head down, in a cup to cool tea quickly.

Sink her all night in a cocktail glass like a swizzle stick.
A girl to stir your drink! Her feet graze its silvered surface.

Plunge her body in. She can swim and spin
in a bath, or you could drown her in your Dirty Martini.

Come on, no harm done, you're just playing a game!

Boys only tease if they like you, I was told.

She won't drown. She's already dead.

Once upon a time on a winter night a young girl named Charlotte did not listen to her mother she rode in a sleigh with her lover to a ball she would not wear the silver wrap her mother offered her mother begged her mother pleaded her mother tried to tie it over her shoulders but Charlotte wanted her pale throat gleaming wanted her arms bare so the sleigh sped through the forest for miles and miles and when the lovers arrived at the village Charlotte was iced and still and white as a wedding cake

Let's speak in praise of the frozen—

My first daughter asleep, her hands pressed flat against my face.

My girls in the bath, underwater, sisters sealed under glass.

On the subway, each time the train tunnels under the river,
how I hold my legs together.
How I hold my breath.

I fold my body up like an umbrella tied too tight.

Need a large amount of Frozen Charlottes?

An orphanage of Frozen Charlottes could be yours for the taking.

You may bid. The reserve is not yet
met. You have one more hour.

Buy huge quantities
of salvaged frozen charlotte dolls
direct from Germany.
75 excavated glazed
Victorian frozen charlotte dolls
size 1–22 inches age 1860.

Current Bid $38.00

How many dolls do you want?

They could be broken, some may have chipped heads,
but these Frozen Charlottes are all clean.

Sold by the gross. Sold by the lot.

Once upon a time, there were dolls, named after a story
meant to teach a lesson—

Once upon a time, between 1850–1920, these dolls were made
in German factories.

Each one inch tall. These girls were perfect insulation

against winter. If a doll was not intact she was stuffed
behind the doll factory wall with her sisters.

All the stories you tell me are so fake, my older daughter says.

sent home from school for wearing open-toed shoes
sent home from school for a halter roped too loosely over my neck
sent home from school because I wore leggings instead of pants
sent home and told to change out of *that too-short skirt*
sent home because of *spaghetti straps*
sent home to my mother because there was *dress code inspection*
and your daughter is not in accordance

Now the mother, I wish for a whalebone corset spun tight—
the always desired 20-inch *wasp waist*—
yet I wish to hold the edges of my mini skirt in my own hands,
to allow whoever I want beneath it.

I loved my t-strap shoes, color of skim milk, shoes only worn on Wednesdays.

At Miggy's Ballroom Dancing Studio, in New Orleans, in 1978, I was taught the foxtrot, the waltz, the cha-cha, the box step. Outside, cars on their way to the Mississippi played The Village People. Cars driven by other, older boys. Girls lined up on one side of the room against the mirrors, boys on the other. And we waited. We'd been told that if a boy asked us to dance the correct answer was always no matter what *yes thank you, yes.*

Penny Dolls
Solid Chinas
Pudding Dolls
Bathing Babies
Pillar Dolls
Living Dead Dolls

Dolls white as gravel scattered in a parking lot

A doll to fit on the surface of a spoon.
Hold her in your mouth—

her body tastes like chalk, bite her thighs, bite her bottom,
and you could choke—

Let's talk about who hid the dolls in ditches, in dry wall,
in rock foundations. Who shoved their bodies hard

inside a wall to keep a factory warm in winter. Who
smashed the dolls together then sealed the wall with plaster?

Kidnapped girls—

Who will find them?

Like survivors after a crash, after a blast,
these girls are always post-earthquake, bodies covered in fine white ash.

the low-rise jeans   crescent of smooth belly

a pink crop top   color of a pencil eraser

the jean skirt made by tearing off both legs

silver bra strap dropped over a shoulder

In praise of white—

Baptismal dress for the babies, linen and itchy, single inherited dress
that made them both cry.

Oyster shells in the parking lot in the bar by the river where I kick up dust.

My wedding dress, skimming my shoulders, *might show too much skin,*
the tailor murmurs in the dressing room.

My half slip, falling over my thighs like a rinse of cool water,
while my older daughter says, *Does anyone still wear those now?*

A muff I loved as a child, cylinder of fur where I stuffed
my fingers so I wouldn't touch myself.

Or how about the disposable mesh underwear
the nurses made me wear
in the hospital
as they wheeled me out after the first surgical birth?

My love, if you find me facedown,

lying in the snow would you save me, would you

pick me up so gently, cradle me, wrap the shawl back

over my shoulders and bring me back to life—

breathe into my lungs

warm my blue skin   my pale mouth

with your own?

Once upon a time the parents of dead Charlotte mourned her and the mother   in grief the mother grew her hair long till it fell past her knees   hair to cloak her   hair the color of eggshell

My daughters are in the bath together   I'm outside

the door   no access to their bodies now

no body

            that will fit now

in the bath with them   so I will myself blank

I close my eyes to white
                              or they're Charlottes—

glazed only on their backs to float

            unclothed

                        face side up

they drift on the surface   ghostly

bodies   sealed in lockets   silent

                        oh my fairy tale dead girls

intrigued I yank the garment from the rack and alone in the store I try on the tight second skin all tight weave no breathing I smooth my black dress flat over my stomach my hipbones will almost show as if I was never a mother why that supreme and terrible pleasure at a knob of bone why that pretense of a body that has never held another

Worn under your clothes! Made to help you disappear!

Steam punk jewelry—*perfect for Frozen Charlottes!*

Just wrap the doll in clock gears, twist copper wire over her hair,

each body the perfect size for a pendant.
Two dolls can be matching earrings that glitter and swing.

Glue a girl to metal backing to make a brooch.

Fill a jelly jar with bodies for future projects!

A doll sealed in a bottle.
A doll in a pocket watch.
A doll on a chain between my breasts.

The girls roll like stone, like marbles, they slip from my fingers, soap in a saucer.

My tiny body doubles. Small and already ruined.

My Penny Babies: my Unblinking, Upright Good Daughters.

Cold and iced and priceless, beloved,

    white as white-out from a tiny bottle my older daughter gives me

    to erase my most recent mistake.

IV.
Of Keeping

Custody or *care* or—

saved in a purse—

not a wallet, clasped shut—

A girl's body?—

Light slashes the window of the room my daughters share.

To keep: *to seize, to hold, to observe, to watch, to await, to take.*

I watch them sleeping.

To care or heed in watching—

the innermost stronghold of a tower.

I want to erase myself—

No—I don't. That's over—

Here it is:

girl after girl after girl—

Acknowledgments

Tupelo Quarterly: "The S&H Green Stamp Book" and "The Mannequin in the Mourning Dress at the Exhibition."

Pleiades: "Object Elegies: My Mother's Bright Green Nylon Panties"; "Object Elegies: Beta Fish"; "Object Elegies: Water Line"; "Object Elegies: Hospital Pain Scale"; "Object Elegies: The Queen of Hearts as Seen by Alice"; "Object Elegies: Rocking Chair"; "Object Elegies: Sippy Cup"; "Object Elegies: Easter Egg."

Chelsea: "The Cocktail, A History" (as "Drinking: A Suite").

Missouri Review, Poem of the Week: "Posture Board, 1820."

New Orleans Review: "Vintage 1969 Baby Tender Love Doll, Talks, Drinks and Wets," "Baby's Cradle, Europe, c. 1810," Breast Pump, c. 1905," "Coral Rattle, 1650," and "Swaddling Band, France, 18th Century."

Indiana Review: "Self-Portrait with Miniatures at the Victoria and Albert Museum."

Drunken Boat: "Object Elegies: Pink Plastic Cake Box," "Object Elegies: English Ironstone Adams China Service for Eight," "Object Elegies: Silver Porringer with Filigree, 1942." "Object Elegies: Quilt with Tatted Border," "Object Elegies: Salt and Pepper Shakers in the Shape of Dutch Girls," "Object Elegies: Souvenir Spoons My Grandmother Collected," "Object Elegies: Ruby Glasses Set of Four," "Object Elegies: Crystal Choker," "Object Elegies: Bag of Diary Keys," and "Object Elegies: A Cocktail Shaker I Plan to Fill with Crayons."

Lumberyard: "Reticule."

Willow Springs: "The Pregnant Doll," "Bye-Lo Baby, Patent Applied For" (as "Bye-Lo Baby, Patent Applied For, Stamped in Black Ink On Her Chest").

Plume: "Booklet, Hand-Pressed Paper, Containing Locks of Schoolchildren's Hair."

"At the Corning Museum of Glass," in *Collecting Life: Poets on Objects Known and Imagined,* eds. Madelyn Garner and Andrea L. Watson.

"The Pregnant Doll," reprinted in *The Doll Collection,* ed. Diane Lockward.

"Frozen Charlottes, A Sequence" originally appeared in a slightly different version as a digital chapbook, Essay Press, 2016.

"Mad Money" (as "Of Nostalgia") appeared as a limited-edition broadside for the Beall Poetry Festival, Baylor University, 2016.

I am grateful to Converse College for awarding several of these poems the Julia Peterkin Award. Gratitude to The New Jersey Arts Council, the PSC-CUNY Award Program from the Research Foundation of the City University of New York, and Queens College-City University of New York for grants that enabled the writing of this book.

Thanks to the first readers of all of my work: Alexander Hinton, Peter Cooley, Jacki Cooley, Alissa Rowan, Kimiko Hahn and Julia Spicher Kasdorf. And I am so grateful to all my friends who have helped and supported me on the journey to this book: Nancy Austin, Amelie Hastie, Roger Sedarat, Maaza Mengiste, Glenn Burger, Talia Schaffer, Timothy Liu, Shelley Renee, Richard Schotter, John Weir and Elizabeth Zervigon.

Thank you to MaryKatherine Callaway, Neal Novak and everyone at LSU Press.

Huge thanks to Ava Leavell Haymon for her editorial brilliance, her humor and her generosity.

Notes

"Mad Money"—A term first coined in the 1920s, mad money is money a girl keeps secretly while on a date in case she has an emergency and needs to go home alone. Also defined as "carfare carried by a girl on a date to provide a means of escaping her escort in the event of unwanted familiarities." *Webster's 3rd Dictionary*, 1961.

"Posture Board, 1820," "Baby's Cradle, Europe, c. 1810," "Breast Pump, c. 1905," "Coral Rattle, 1650" and "Swaddling Band, France, 18th Century"—All of the objects here are exhibited at the Victoria and Albert Museum of Childhood, Bethanel Green, London.

"From My Mother's Copy of Peg Bracken's *I Hate to Cook Book* (1960)—This poem uses language from writer Peg Bracken's recipes in her books on cooking and housekeeping.

"The Mannequin in the Mourning Dress at the Exhibition"—Some language here is taken from commentary by Harold Koda and Jessica Regan, co-curators at the Costume Institute at the Metropolitan Museum, for the exhibit titled "Her: A Century of Mourning Attire" as well as from Walker R. Houghton et al *American Etiquette and Rules of Politeness*, 1889.

"Reticule"—This poem is sparked by the exhibit "Clutch It! The Purse and the Person" at The Seattle Museum of History and Industry.

"Bye-Lo Baby, Patent Applied For"—In the 1920s, artist and doll designer Grace S. Putnam wanted to design the most life-like doll possible so she visited newborns in nurseries at the hospital to study their features.

"Resurrection Cake"—This poem is written in memory of my grandmother, Anne Marks.

"Frozen Charlottes, A Sequence"—The quoted material here is taken from Kay Desmonde, *Dolls and Doll Houses;* Saba Smith, "Fair Charlotte" (1840); *The New York Observer* (1840); and eBay.

"The Pregnant Doll"—This doll is exhibited in the Victoria and Albert Museum of Childhood, Bethanel Green, London.